NEW SUBWAYS

Proposed Additions to Rapid Transit System to Cost $218,000,000

TRANSIT COMMISSION

GEORGE MCANENY, Chairman

LEROY T. HARKNESS JOHN F. O'RYAN

JAMES B. WALKER, Secretary

49 LAFAYETTE STREET
NEW YORK

May, 1922

NEW RAPID TRANSIT RAILROADS

Statement by Transit Commission

PROVISION for the building of new subways is one of the most important of the duties with which the Transit Commission is charged. The orders issued, or to be issued by the Commission for increasing service on the existing lines as rapidly as the financial condition of the operating companies permits will, for the time being, afford a substantial degree of relief. But these measures are palliatives only, and do not solve the problem. The growth of the rapid transit traffic, which increases daily, has been upon an enormous scale. The new lines provided under the dual contracts, which more than doubled the mileage of the original subway and elevated system, have been open but a few years, and are already crowded to capacity.

A comparison of the number of passengers carried under the highly congested conditions of 1913—the year in which the dual contract construction was commenced—with the number carried in 1921, with the dual system not yet completed, shows that, within eight years, rapid transit traffic, subway and elevated, has nearly doubled. The figures are as follows:

	Passengers Carried 1913	1921
	(Fiscal Year Ending June 30)	
(1) INTERBOROUGH COMPANY		
(a) Subway lines	327,471,510	639,385,780
(b) Manhattan elevated lines ...	306,845,006	374,293,051
	634,316,516	1,013,678,831
(2) BROOKLYN RAPID TRANSIT COMPANIES		
(a) Subway lines	....	175,431,045
(b) Elevated lines of the Kings County system linked with the subway under the dual contracts	162,514,055	229,539,595
	162,514,055	404,970,640
(3) TOTAL RAPID TRANSIT TRAFFIC	796,830,571	1,418,649,471

Figures like these tell their own story. They show, chiefly, the enormous trend toward the subways, where the total figure of 327,000,000 carried in 1913—when the Interborough Company was the sole subway operator—has risen to 815,000,000 on the dual system in 1921, an increase of 250 per cent.

At the same time, and notwithstanding this vast increase in the number of subway riders, the traffic of the elevated lines not only held its own, but also increased, from 469,000,000 to 603,000,000, or 30 per cent.

The increase on subway and elevated lines combined, through this brief period, was 80 per cent—with the growth of the fiscal year about to end yet to be counted.

Relief Required

During the rush hours the lines of both companies are carrying very nearly the maximum number of trains their trackage will accommodate. Bringing in more cars, as the Commission's service orders require, "spreading the peak" of the period of worst congestion, and keying up the service in every possible respect will continue to help; but points of "saturation" will again be reached, long before new lines are ready for use. The building of new lines offers, in fact, the only means of permanent and continuous relief, and it is the conviction of the Commission that a broad building program should be launched with the least possible delay.

A building program should have been under way five years ago. Not a new line has been provided, however, since March of 1913, and some of the construction work then required by the dual contracts has not yet been finished.

The time consumed in the building of a subway, including the laying out and validation of routes, the drawing of plans, the preparation of contracts and the actual construction work runs from three to five years.

New Lines and Routes

With such time demands in view, the Commission took up the matter of necessary new construction shortly after its appointment. It has since had under consideration a variety of routes and plans, studied out and prepared, in the first instance, by its Consulting Engineer, Daniel L. Turner, and from among these, has agreed upon seven major projects as the first to be presented. It will proceed with the formal adoption of the particular routes included, and take whatever other steps are necessary to set the actual work in motion, as soon as opportunity has been given for full public discussion.

The separate lines proposed, listed in the order in which the Commission believes they should be put under construction, are as follows:

I. The extension of the Corona Line, in North Queens, from Corona to Flushing.

II. The extension of the cross-town subway in Forty-second Street, Manhattan, with moving platform or other auxiliary equipment, connecting with each of the present and future north and south rapid transit lines, both subway and elevated.

III. A Staten Island Tunnel, to connect with the Fourth Avenue Subway, in Brooklyn, and with the various steam and trolley lines in Staten Island.

IV. An extension of the Broadway-Seventh Avenue Line of the Brooklyn Rapid Transit system, from Fifty-ninth Street, Manhattan, under Central Park West, 110th Street and Seventh Avenue to 155th Street.

V. A Brooklyn crosstown line from the Queensborough Plaza in Long Island City to a point of connection with the Brighton Beach Line, at or near Franklin Avenue and Fulton Street, Brooklyn.

VI. A new subway and East River tunnel to connect the Fulton Street Elevated Line, in Brooklyn, with the Broadway-Fourth Avenue Line, at the City Hall station, in Manhattan.

VII. A new trunk line subway to run from downtown, Manhattan, to Washington Heights, following, in the main, Eighth and Amsterdam Avenues.

Concurrent Construction

Although a certain order of construction is indicated, it is the judgment of the Commission that, so far as possible, the preliminary work upon all of these lines should be taken up at once, and without material difference in the fixing of the dates of actual beginning of construction. It is considered equally important that the entire program should be arranged, so far as possible, in construction units that will be capable of immediate operation as integral parts of the transit system, each as soon as it can be completed, thereby avoiding waste either in the use of operable structures, or in the unnecessary accumulation of interest. The plans of the engineers have been worked out with these ends in view.

The details of the routes proposed, with the estimated costs and periods of time for construction are as follows:

Flushing Extension

(1) The line to Flushing which, some years ago, was assured first place in the program of extensions to the dual system, will run as a three track continuation of the elevated structure from Corona to Flushing Creek, and from thence as a two track subway to Main Street. It will cross the creek on a drawbridge, the plans for which are about to be submitted for approval to the War Department, and at its terminal will connect with practically all of the trolley lines entering Flushing from the north.

The estimated cost of the work is $2,800,000, and the time of completion three and a half years.

Across Forty-second Street

(2) The 42nd Street line would, if equipped with moving platforms, carried in subways under the present sidewalks, be ready for use in three years, and would cost, including station finish, track and real estate, $6,000,000.

From a traffic point of view the 42nd Street problem is, next to Canal Street, the most important now pressing for solution. The present shuttle service, as the cross-bar in the "H" system, has far outgrown its temporary purpose and should be replaced as soon as possible. Passengers are now required to walk a quarter of a mile between the shuttle, with two intervals of waiting, one for the shuttle itself, and one for the uptown or downtown train. The unloading, simultaneously, of an entire trainload of passengers causes intolerable crowding on the mainline platforms, and aggravates the discomforts of delay. The Commission believes that the device of the moving platform might provide all of the transfer facilities needed perhaps more satisfactorily than any other method. It would reduce walking to a minimum; give continuous service instead of intermittent; shorten the time of transfer; do away with the congestion due to mass arrivals; increase capacity, and provide seats for everyone.

Carried from river to river, this service incidentally, will solve another serious transit problem. There are seven rapid transit trunk lines, subway and elevated, with twenty-three tracks, at present routing across 42nd Street uptown and downtown, without connection with or transfer to a single crosstown line. When the Eighth Avenue line is built, there will be four more such tracks. This is a vital defect in the carrying system as it exists today. There should be a number of crosstown lines, to give proper convenience and elasticity to the general Manhattan system, but the most pressing need, no doubt, is that existing at 42nd Street, and this need, too, would be met by a moving platform. As a further gain, the present surface railroad could be eliminated, and proper connection afforded at the 42nd Street North River Ferry for the suburban traffic received at that point. The Commission, having in view possible alternatives, is also reserving appropriate levels for the building of additional subway tracks across 42nd Street, when and if they are required. It also has under consideration the possible desirability of connecting part of the 42nd Street line on a loop plan with a new crosstown line through the 34th Street district.

Staten Island Tunnel

(3) For the connection to Staten Island two alternatives are offered. That at present favored by the Commission would be provided by the building of a two track subway, beginning at Fourth Avenue and 67th Street, the present terminus of the Fourth Avenue line in Brooklyn, running through Fourth Avenue under private property and the Ridge Boulevard to Fort Hamilton, and thence under the Narrows to Pennsylvania Avenue, in Staten Island. Via Pennsylvania Avenue the tunnel would extend to a point near Vermont Avenue, at which connection can be made to the South Beach branch of the Staten Island Rapid Transit Railway, continuing thence through Pennsylvania Avenue to the South Side Boulevard, where connection can also be made to Tottenville, and other points now reached through the trolley system.

Such a subway and tunnel would take from five to five and a half years to build. The engineers of the Commission, however, also recommend that, upon the completion of the line to Fort Hamilton, a Municipal Ferry be put in operation to connect with the Staten

Island points. Such a ferry would cost $3,000,000, and would bring the island traffic in touch with the general subway system three years earlier. Upon the completion of the entire line, it would still find a highly useful service in providing a crossing point for vehicular traffic.

The alternative Staten Island route proposed would begin at Fourth Avenue and 67th Street, Brooklyn, at a connection with the Fourth Avenue line, and proceed under New York Bay to Arietta Street, in Staten Island, where connection would be made with the rapid transit and trolley systems.

To complete the Fort Hamilton route, subway and tunnel, would cost approximately $17,000,000, with $3,000,000 added if a ferry service is used. The route to Arietta Street, while having a balancing advantage in touching more directly the Staten Island communities at present the most populous, would cost about $4,000,000 more.

It is appreciated that the Board of Estimate and Apportionment, under a legislative act of 1921, has been preparing to construct a tunnel connection between Brooklyn and Staten Island, for the joint use of passenger and freight traffic. So far as such a tunnel is designed to carry rapid transit passengers, it would, of course, be essential that it be planned in cooperation with the Transit Commission. The engineers of the Commission are, however, unanimous in their judgment that a tunnel designed to carry freight trains cannot be used for rapid transit passenger purposes. In this judgment the engineers of the Board of Estimate have apparently concurred; though the Commission has not as yet been informed of the nature or extent of their present plans. The Commission is, of course, prepared to enter into any manner of practicable cooperation that will give the Borough of Richmond its much needed transit relief.

The Transit Construction Commissioner, predecessor of the Transit Commission, initiated the preparation of plans for a rapid transit tunnel as early as May, 1920, at which time an appropriation of $50,000 was made by the Board of Estimate and Apportionment to provide for the incidental surveys and explorations necessary to the development of more detailed designs and the selection of a place for the proper tunnel crossing. At the time of the passage of the Act of 1921 this work had been advanced considerably, but it was stopped when the Board of Estimate cut out the appropriation covering it, which the Transit Commission had inherited. It seems not improbable that if the Fort Hamilton Route be chosen, a plan might be agreed upon under which the freight and rapid transit tunnels can be built at the same time, with a consequent saving in the net cost of each.

Broadway Subway Extension

(4) The Broadway-Fourth Avenue Line, now operated by the Brooklyn Rapid Transit Company to 59th Street, Manhattan, is a four track trunk line running from 86th Street and Fourth Avenue, in Brooklyn, over and under the East River by way of Manhattan Bridge and the Whitehall Tunnel, and via Broadway and Seventh Avenue, North. The southern terminal of this line is already supplied with more branches than the trunk tracks can properly accomodate, but the northern extremity has but one collecting and distributing branch, the two track line through 59th and 60th Streets to the Queensborough Plaza. The other two tracks of the trunk line are dead-ended at 59th Street. For this reason, workward in the morning and homeward at night, during the rush hours, only half of the capacity of the line is developed from the northern terminal. Passengers using the Brooklyn system are, moreover, unable to pass north of 59th Street without paying an additional fare at an Interborough station.

It is proposed, therefore, to build another two track extension from Seventh Avenue North under Central Park West, and the Park to 110th Street, and thence via Seventh Avenue to 155th Street and Eighth Avenue. A spur track for such a connection has already been constructed. This extension would provide, in effect, another north and south line for the full length of Manhattan Island. It would relieve very materially the Ninth and Sixth Avenue Lines of the Manhattan Elevated Company, as well as the Lenox Avenue branch of the original subway between 110th Street and the Harlem River.

Furthermore, it would hasten the time when the Sixth Avenue elevated line may be removed from the street. This line at present adds practically nothing to the capacity of the city's rapid transit facilities. It adds only to the convenience of the passengers using it, and its removal from the street would provide the most immediate outlet possible for the sort of development that is now overstraining Fifth Avenue.

Another incidental advantage of this extension would be that the surface tracks upon Central Park West may be more readily removed—as the subway would provide virtually the same service—and the released surface of the street thereupon transformed into a westerly Park Boulevard.

The approximate cost of the Central Park West-Seventh Avenue extension would be $26,500,000, and the time consumed in construction three and one-half years.

Brooklyn Crosstown Line

(5) The so-called Brooklyn Crosstown Line was originally projected as an elevated when the dual system was laid out, but its construction was deferred because of local objection to elevated construction, and because of the fact that the city's resources for the more expensive alternative of subway building had been ex-

hausted. It is the opinion of the Commission that the line should be built as a subway without further delay —first, as a means of articulating all of the rapid transit lines at present traversing Brooklyn and Queens, so that any one of these can be reached conveniently and quickly from any other one; second, as a means of access to the shore front of Brooklyn and Queens north of the Navy Yard; and third, as a direct means of carrying passengers from Manhattan and Queens to Brooklyn and Coney Island without traversing the congested district of lower Manhattan.

Such a line will tend further to decentralize traffic by building up another prosperous business thoroughfare north and south in Brooklyn, and will save the Queens traffic bound for Brooklyn from a long detour through Manhattan.

Through Long Island City the line will follow Jackson Avenue, one of the widest and most important thoroughfares in the business section of Queens. Through the Greenpoint section of Brooklyn, it will follow Manhattan Avenue, the principal business street of that section, and thence through Roebling Street, Williamsburgh, and by the cutting of a new street, of about three blocks in length, from Roebling Street to Bedford Avenue, to a connection with the Brighton Beach Line at Fulton Street and Franklin Avenue. In its progress it would furnish points of transfer to the stations of all the other lines it would intercept—the Broadway, Myrtle and Lexington Avenue elevated lines, and the 14th Street-Eastern subway.

The Commission has also in view a further connection between this line by way of Flushing Avenue or Park Avenue and Jay and Smith Streets, to the Borough Hall section of Brooklyn. At some future time, no doubt, it will also be desirable to connect the northern end of the line directly with the Astoria branch of the Queensborough system, thence into Manhattan at 125th Street and across 125th Street to Fort Lee Ferry.

The estimated cost of the line as now proposed is $24,000,000., and the time to complete from three to three and one-half years.

Central Brooklyn Line

(6) The proposed link between the Fulton Street elevated line in Brooklyn and the Manhattan sections of the Brooklyn Rapid Transit subway would proceed, at the Brooklyn end, by way of the so-called "Ashland Place connection." This will provide additionally a connection with the present Fourth Avenue Subway. It is the view of the Commission, however, that another crossing to Manhattan should be afforded through a new East River tunnel, for the relief from over-crowding of the existing Whitehall tunnel. If such a plan is followed, it will involve more or less modification of the Nassau Street Line in Manhattan. The building of this line, for which provision is made in the dual contracts, had not been undertaken, apparently more or less by common consent, during the eight years preceding 1921.

The present Commission, upon its appointment a year ago, made no change in this situation, pending proper consideration of plans under which it might be linked with a tunnel of its own or otherwise modified. The present recommendations of the Commission's engineers cover two alternative routes. Each of these would require, at the start, the removal of the elevated railroad from lower Fulton Street, Brooklyn, thereby greatly improving the most important thoroughfare of that borough. Under either, the Fulton Street tracks would be dropped to a subway at a point at or near Clermont Avenue, and carried thence via Fulton Street, private property, Fort Greene Place, DeKalb Avenue, further private property and Livingston Street to Sidney Place. From this point, the first of the alternative routes would proceed under Grace Court and the East River to Nassau Street, and thence across Park

Row under the present Post Office Building to a connection with the Broadway Subway at City Hall, Manhattan. Under the second alternative, the line would run from Livingston Street under private property to Clinton Street, and thence through Liberty Street and lower Fulton Street under the East River to Ann Street, in Manhattan, and across Park Row to the main line at City Hall.

The great Central District of Brooklyn has so far been deprived of proper access to the city wide subway system. The Commission wishes to right this seeming injustice as soon as possible. Brooklyn needs more than anything else in the way of transit facilities additional trunk line access to and through Manhattan. There are so many branch lines traversing the Borough of Brooklyn under the dual plan, the traffic upon all of which is developing remarkably, and so few trunk lines serving these, that only about half of the full capacity of the existing Brooklyn system can really be developed until more trunk lines are constructed. This, in the judgment of the Commission, is the strongest argument in favor of the construction of a new and separate tunnel for the downtown Manhattan connections.

The estimated cost of the first of the alternatives proposed from Ashland Place to the City Hall, within which part of the original Nassau Street line would be incorporated, is $28,000,000, and that of the Ann Street connection, $25,000,000. In estimating the outlay upon either of these alternatives, however, allowance should be made for the estimated cost of $7,000,000 of the Nassau line as a link in the dual plan, which is still carried in the estimates of uncompleted dual work, and which, of course, would be deducted from the total cost of the purely new work.

Eighth Avenue-Amsterdam Avenue Subway

(7) The Eighth Avenue-Amsterdam Avenue line would, in many respects, be the most important and the

most ambitious in scope. Beginning at a point in Forty-first Street between Seventh and Eighth Avenues, where direct physical connection is to be made with the Queensborough subway, ground for which was broken recently, it will run south on a four track line through Eighth Avenue to Fourteenth Street, and as a two track line to Hudson and Chambers Streets. Northward from Forty-first Street it will run as a four track subway up Eighth Avenue and across Fifty-seventh Street, with underground access to Columbus Circle, and up Amsterdam Avenue to 103rd Street, thence as a four track subway to 155th Street, still via Amsterdam Avenue but as a three track subway to 159th Street and Fort Washington Avenue, and thence to 181st Street.

It is proposed to construct the Eighth Avenue line by sections, each capable of linking up upon its completion with some part of the transit system now in use, and in accordance with the following program:

(a) The first section recommended for construction will cover the portion of the line extending from 41st Street to Fourteenth. This will carry four tracks, but so placed as to permit the addition of another group of tracks at a later date. Eventually eight tracks are designed for the full trunk sections of this route. Those now to be built will be located in a two deck four track subway, placed on the west side of the avenue. At Forty-first Street this will be connected with the Queensborough extension, and at 14th Street—by means of two connecting tracks to Sixth Avenue and Fourteenth Street—with the Fourteenth Street-Eastern line, to Brooklyn.

These connections will afford a through loop service between the Queensborough and 14th Street lines, incidentally opening up one of the most important sections of Manhattan to either.

(b) The second building stage, south on Eighth Avenue and Hudson Street, will carry the line from Fourteenth Street to the terminal at Chambers Street, where passengers desiring to go further south in Manhattan, or to Brooklyn, will transfer to the Broadway-Seventh Avenue line.

(c) The third step will cover the section north, again as a two deck four track subway, on the westerly side of Eighth Avenue to Fifty-seventh Street, and thence by way of Amsterdam Avenue to 103rd Street. At this point, the traffic of the Lenox Avenue branch of the existing subway can be diverted to the new line, thereby providing for the immediate relief of the upper west side of Manhattan through the turning over of the existing Broadway-Seventh Avenue line entirely to its service.

(d) As a fourth and final step, the line will be continued on a four track single level up Amsterdam Avenue to 155th Street, and from this point, with three tracks, up Fort Washington Avenue to 181st Street. This fourth unit will provide the further facilities so badly needed through the densely built apartment territory that has developed in upper Manhattan, as the result of the building of the first subway. It would provide this territory with an express service beginning at 155th Street and running the full distance south to Fourteenth Street.

The estimated cost of the Eighth Avenue line by sections would be: (a) $12,000,000; (b) $7,500,000; (c) $24,000,000; (d) $26,000,000—a total of $69,500,000. Sections (a) and (b) would take a little over three years to complete; section (c) and (d), four years.

Concourse at Columbus Circle

It is proposed, incidentally, to develop a general concourse station at Columbus Circle, where the lines of the Amsterdam Avenue, the Broadway-Central Park West connection and the present subway will converge, all within an area of two or three blocks. This would bring the service of practically every part of the City to Columbus Circle and materially stimulate the development of this increasingly important section of Manhattan.

While the building of the Amsterdam Avenue line to Washington Heights, and the extension of the Broadway line to Harlem, will provide the west side of Manhattan for some time to come with the facilities it so badly requires, the crosstown line through Brooklyn, connecting with all of Manhattan north of the Queensborough Bridge connection, will greatly relieve the present pressure on the east side lines. The provision made at various points in the new plan for cross connections, affecting nearly every line in the city, will in turn permit a much improved distribution of the general traffic, and aid the better development of the city itself.

Mileage and Cost

The several new routes projected will add the following track and route mileage to the present mileage of the dual system:—

No.	Classification	Length of Route in Miles	Length of Tracks in Miles
1.	Flushing Extension	1.90	5.20
2.	42nd Street Cross-town Line	2.00	4.00
3.	Staten Island Tunnel; Either alternative	3.20	6.40
4.	Central Park West-7th Avenue Extension	5.40	12.50
5.	Brooklyn Crosstown Line	6.25	12.50
6.	Fulton Street Elevated Extension	2.80	5.60
7.	Eighth Avenue - Amsterdam Avenue Line	11.00	38.00
	Totals,	32.55	84.20

The total estimated cost of the construction of the seven projects in view is in round numbers $174,000,000. With the addition to this figure of the overhead costs of administration and engineering, and the amounts of interest paid during construction on the funds employed —estimated at $44,000,000 in all—the total cost of the lines will be $218,000,000.

The funds necessary to meet the cost of construction will, no doubt, be raised, as required, through the sale of city bonds. The methods for providing the amounts required for the equipment of the new lines, which may reach an additional $100,000,000, will be determined as the general consideration of the future relationship of the city and the operating companies proceeds. The degree to which bonds for construction may be sold under the city's present constitutional margin of borrowing capacity is yet to be determined. The Commission understands from the official statements of the city Comptroller that a substantial borrowing margin is already available. It will, however, very naturally consult both the Comptroller and the Board of Estimate upon the general subject of financing at the appropriate time.

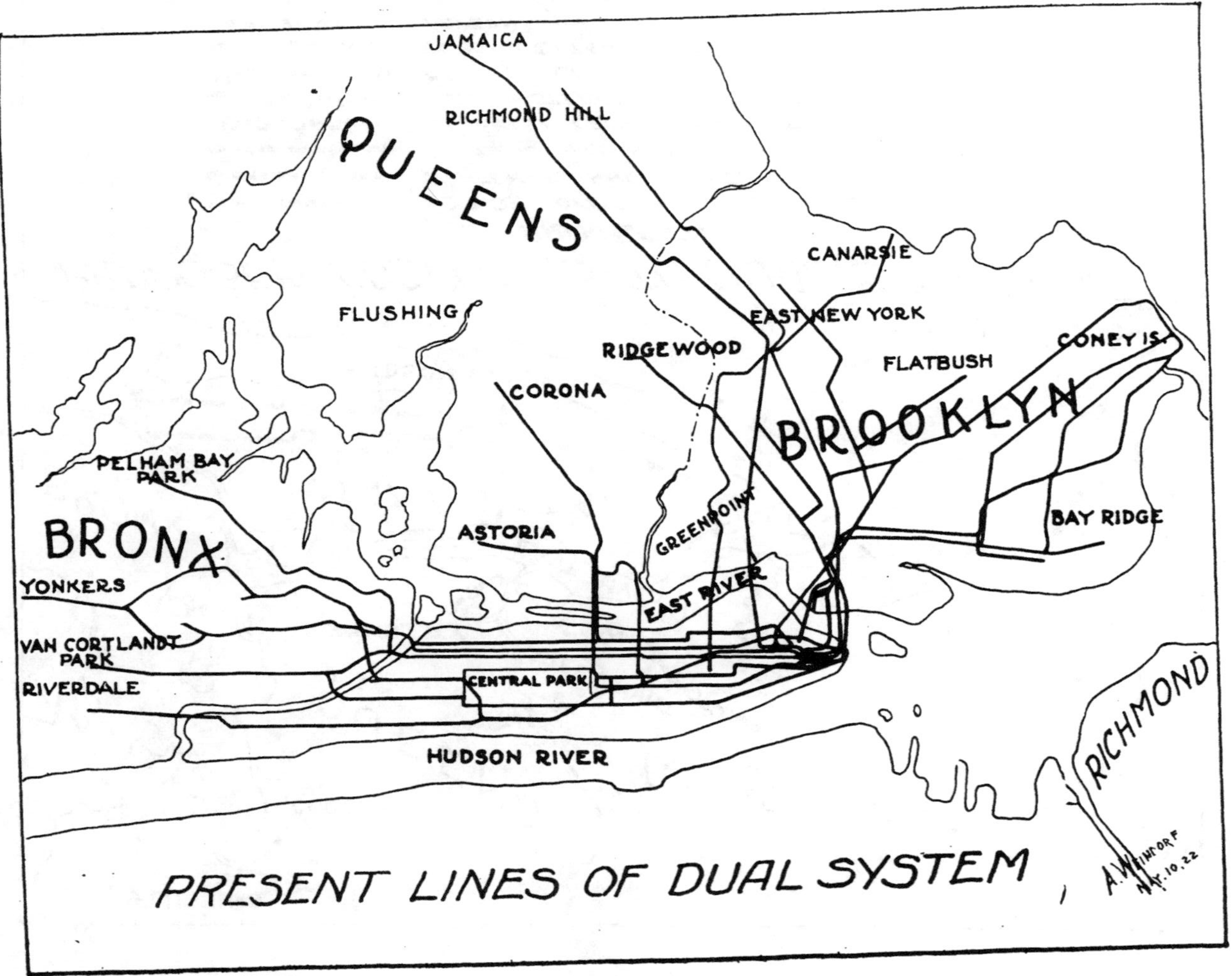
JAMAICA
RICHMOND HILL
QUEENS
FLUSHING
CANARSIE
EAST NEW YORK
RIDGEWOOD
FLATBUSH
CONEY IS.
CORONA
BROOKLYN
PELHAM BAY PARK
BRONX
ASTORIA
GREENPOINT
BAY RIDGE
YONKERS
EAST RIVER
VAN CORTLANDT PARK
RIVERDALE
CENTRAL PARK
RICHMOND
HUDSON RIVER
PRESENT LINES OF DUAL SYSTEM

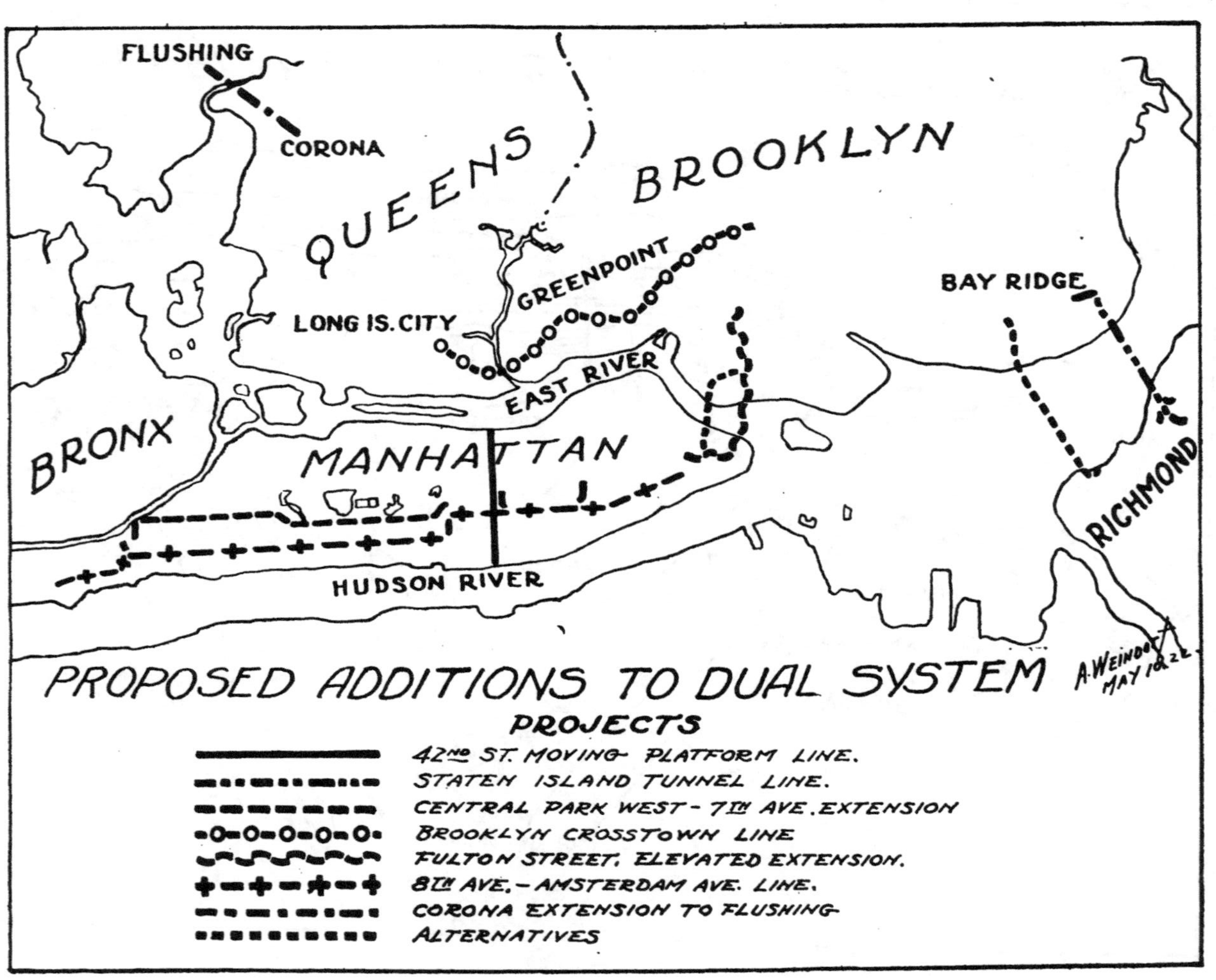
FLUSHING
CORONA
QUEENS
BROOKLYN
LONG IS. CITY
GREENPOINT
BAY RIDGE
EAST RIVER
BRONX
MANHATTAN
RICHMOND
HUDSON RIVER
A. WEINDORF MAY 1922
PROPOSED ADDITIONS TO DUAL SYSTEM
PROJECTS
42ND ST. MOVING PLATFORM LINE.
STATEN ISLAND TUNNEL LINE.
CENTRAL PARK WEST - 7TH AVE. EXTENSION
BROOKLYN CROSSTOWN LINE
FULTON STREET, ELEVATED EXTENSION.
8TH AVE. - AMSTERDAM AVE. LINE.
CORONA EXTENSION TO FLUSHING
ALTERNATIVES

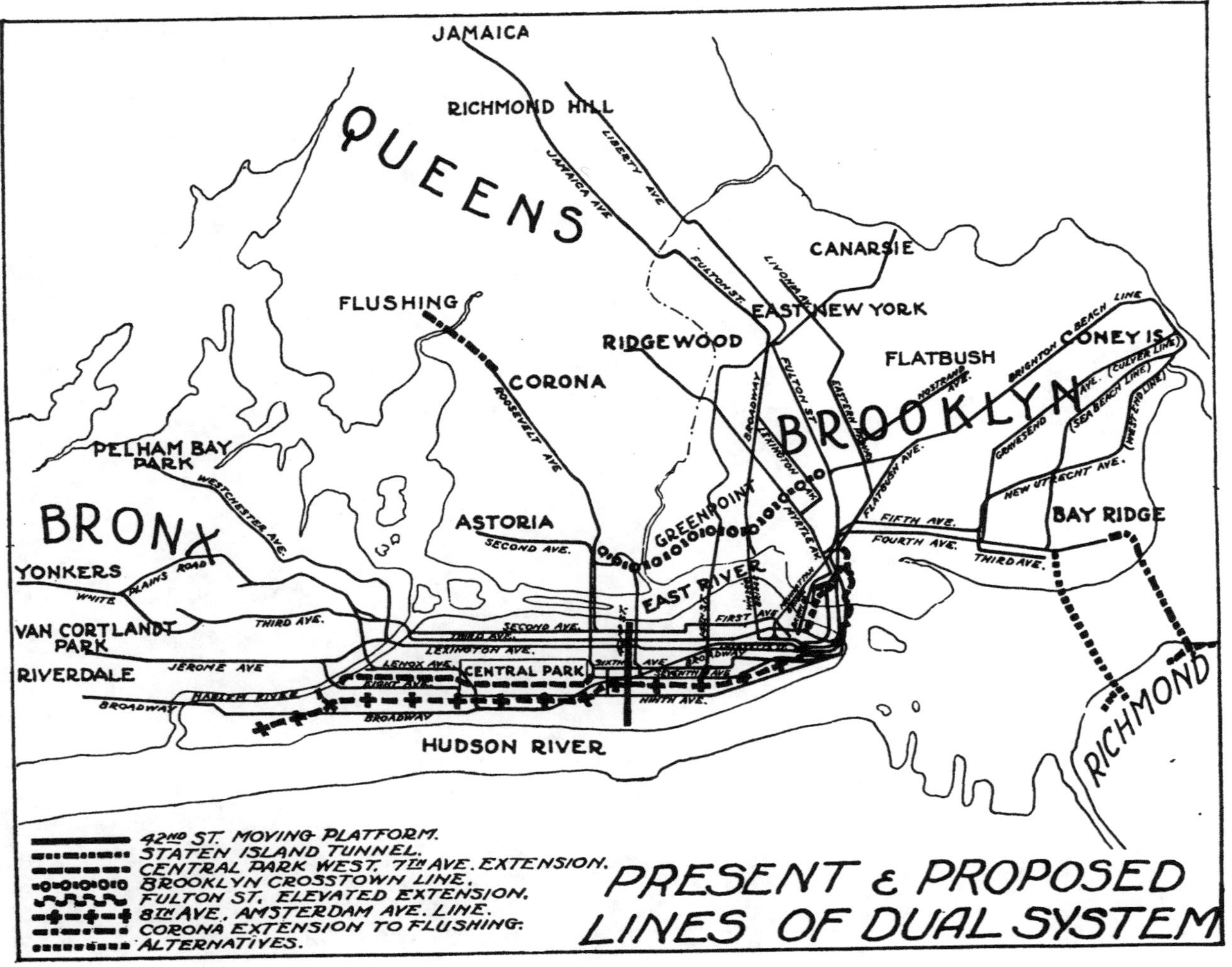
JAMAICA
RICHMOND HILL
QUEENS
LIBERTY AVE
JAMAICA AVE
CANARSIE
FULTON ST.
EAST NEW YORK
FLUSHING
RIDGEWOOD
FLATBUSH
CONEY IS.
BRIGHTON BEACH LINE
CORONA
ROOSEVELT AVE
BROOKLYN
EASTERN PARKWAY
PELHAM BAY PARK
WESTCHESTER AVE.
GRAVESEND AVE. (CULVER LINE)
(SEA BEACH LINE)
NEW UTRECHT AVE.
BRONX
ASTORIA
SECOND AVE.
GREENPOINT
BAY RIDGE
FIFTH AVE.
FOURTH AVE.
THIRD AVE.
YONKERS
WHITE PLAINS ROAD
EAST RIVER
VAN CORTLANDT PARK
THIRD AVE.
SECOND AVE.
FIRST AVE.
LEXINGTON AVE.
RIVERDALE
JEROME AVE
LENOX AVE.
CENTRAL PARK
SIXTH AVE
SEVENTH AVE
BROADWAY
HARLEM RIVER
NINTH AVE.
BROADWAY
HUDSON RIVER
RICHMOND
42ND ST. MOVING PLATFORM.
STATEN ISLAND TUNNEL.
CENTRAL PARK WEST. 7TH AVE. EXTENSION.
BROOKLYN CROSSTOWN LINE.
FULTON ST. ELEVATED EXTENSION.
8TH AVE. AMSTERDAM AVE. LINE.
CORONA EXTENSION TO FLUSHING.
ALTERNATIVES.
PRESENT & PROPOSED
LINES OF DUAL SYSTEM

www.ingramcontent.com/pod-product-compliance
Lightning Source LLC
LaVergne TN
LVHW011147110826
845150LV00008B/2563

* 9 7 8 1 4 1 8 1 9 3 5 4 6 *